The Revolutionary War

VOLUME 6

The Revolutionary War

VOLUME 6
The Road to Valley Forge

James R. Arnold & Roberta Wiener

GROLIER

An imprint of

■SCHOLASTIC

Scholastic Library Publishing

www.scholastic.com/librarypublishing

First published 2001 by Grolier
An imprint of Scholastic Library Publishing
Old Sherman Turnpike
Danbury, Connecticut 06816

For information address the publisher:
Scholastic Library Publishing, Old Sherman Turnpike,
Danbury, Connecticut 06816

Reprinted in 2006

Library of Congress Cataloging-in-Publication Data

The Revolutionary War.
    p. cm.
  Contents: v. 1. The road to rebellion—v. 2. The shot heard around
the world—v. 3. Taking up arms—v. 4. The spirit of 1776—v. 5.
1777: A year of decision—v. 6. The road to Valley Forge—v. 7. War of
attrition—v. 8. The American cause in peril—v. 9. The turn of the tide
—v. 10. An independent nation.
    Includes bibliographical references and indexes.
    ISBN 0-7172-5553-0 (set)—ISBN 0-7172-5554-9 (v. 1)—
ISBN 0-7172-5555-7 (v. 2)—ISBN 0-7172-5556-5 (v. 3)—
ISBN 0-7172-5557-3 (v. 4)—ISBN 0-7172-5558-1 (v. 5)—
ISBN 0-7172-5559-X (v. 6)—ISBN 0-7172-5560-3 (v. 7)—
ISBN 0-7172-5561-1 (v. 8)—ISBN 0-7172-5562-X (v. 9)—
ISBN 0-7172-5563-8 (v. 10)
    1. United States—History—Revolution, 1775–1783—Juvenile
literature. [1. united States—History—Revolution. 1775–1783.]
I. Grolier Incorporated.
E208 .R47   2002   8988
973.3—dc21   2001018998

Printed and bound in Singapore

CONTENTS

CHAPTER ONE

Washington and Howe

*For the main American and British armies the 1776
campaign season ended after the Battle of Princeton.
Along with the Battle of Trenton (December 26, 1776),
Princeton (January 3, 1777) was a wonderful
American victory. During both battles George
Washington had led his army with skill.*

Military experts understood that successful generals
used certain laws, or principles, of war. For the
first time, at Trenton and Princeton Washington showed
that he understood some of the principles of war. He
had fought an attacking campaign, or an offensive. In
order to attack, Washington had marched his army
quickly in ways that the British generals did not expect.
In military language he had used the principle of
maneuver. His attack against the Hessians at Trenton
and the British at Princeton had surprised his enemies.
So, Washington had combined the principles of
offensive, maneuver, and surprise.

Before Trenton and Princeton many people on both
sides doubted that Washington was a very good general.
After all, Washington had made many mistakes during
the 1776 campaign and suffered serious losses. After
Trenton and Princeton people saw that Washington was
a capable general. A newspaper, the Pennsylvania
Journal, wrote: "Washington retreats like a General and
acts like a hero." Such praise was important.
Washington needed to recruit a new army for 1777, and
men would not join his army if they thought that
Washington was a bad general.

George Washington's leadership during the Trenton and Princeton campaigns impressed people both in America and in Europe.

After Princeton Washington led his army to Morristown, New Jersey. In the Revolutionary War large armies in the middle and northern colonies did not campaign (march and fight battles) during the winter. Mud and snow often blocked the poor roads. The heavy wagons that carried an army's supplies could barely move. If the soldiers camped outside in the cold and wet winter weather, many got sick. For those reasons generals usually did not want to risk their armies in a winter campaign. Instead, the armies went into winter quarters.

Washington chose Morristown for his winter quarters in 1776–77. The main British army was around New York City. Washington thought that when spring came, the British would either march up the Hudson River or move south against the American capital at Philadelphia. By keeping his army at Morristown, Washington was in a position to move his army to block, or intercept, either move.

Washington's biggest challenge was to form a large enough army in time to fight the British in the spring of 1777. The heart and soul of the American army (also called the rebel, the patriot, or the Continental army) was the regular or continental soldier. The continentals' terms of enlistment (the amount of time a soldier agreed to serve in the army) ended while the army was at Morristown. Most of the continentals went home.

In Philadelphia Congress had voted to raise a new continental army to replace the men who went home. But the new soldiers were slow to gather. Washington warned, "The campaign is opening, and we have no men for the field." When spring came, Washington divided the forces that he did have into four groups. Washington's small army stayed in New Jersey to watch the British in New York. Another force was in the Hudson Highlands. Its job was to prevent the British

Washington's headquarters at Morristown

from moving north up the Hudson River. Farther north 2,500 Continentals guarded Fort Ticonderoga. In the Mohawk Valley 450 Continentals protected Fort Stanwix. The two forts guarded the north against a British invasion from Canada.

Washington did not know the exact British plan, or strategy, for 1777. All he could do was wait for the British to begin their campaign. In other words, the American forces would be on the defensive (defending their positions) while the British would be on the offensive (attacking the Americans).

The British Strategy for 1777

The man who commanded all of the British army forces in North America was General William Howe. During most of 1776 Howe had achieved one victory after another. He had defeated Washington during the New York Campaign (see Volume 4). By December 20, 1776, one of Howe's generals, Lord Charles Cornwallis, had conquered most of New Jersey. At that time, thousands

A soldier in the 2nd New York Continental Line

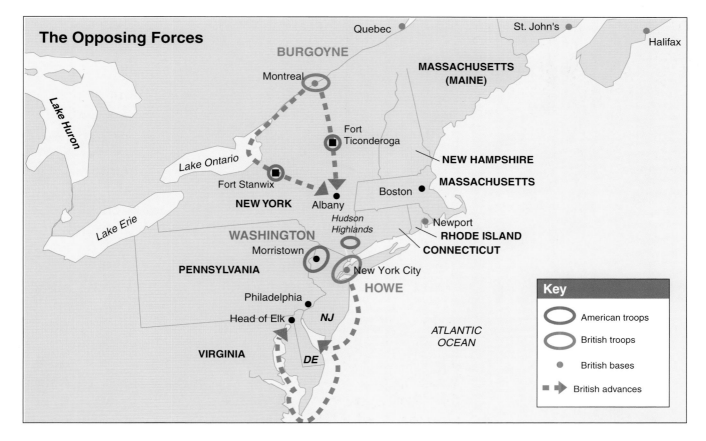

The Opposing Forces

Quebec •   St. John's •   Halifax •

BURGOYNE

Montreal

MASSACHUSETTS (MAINE)

Lake Huron

Lake Ontario

Fort Ticonderoga

Fort Stanwix

NEW YORK   Albany

Lake Erie

NEW HAMPSHIRE

MASSACHUSETTS

Boston •

Hudson Highlands

WASHINGTON

Morristown

PENNSYLVANIA

Philadelphia •

Head of Elk •

• Newport

RHODE ISLAND

CONNECTICUT

New York City

HOWE

NJ

ATLANTIC OCEAN

VIRGINIA   *DE*

Key	
⬭	American troops
⬭	British troops
•	British bases
▪▪▶	British advances

of New Jersey loyalists (people loyal to the king, also called Tories) were helping the British. Howe waited in New York City for news that the war was almost won.

Instead came the two surprise attacks at Trenton and Princeton. Because of the rebel attacks the British abandoned most of New Jersey. The New Jersey loyalists who were helping the British had to return home to defend their property against the rebels. For all of his effort during 1776 Howe was left only with the area around New York City, a small foothold in New Jersey at New Brunswick and Perth Amboy, and the port of Newport in Rhode Island.

Still, New York City and Newport were valuable. In 1776 Howe had to capture a base before beginning his campaign. In 1777 he already had two safe bases and could begin a campaign as soon as the winter ended. In other words, Howe could get a much earlier start. The question that he and the British leaders back in London had to answer was where to attack.

On June 14, 1777, a congressional committee resolved "that the flag of the United States be thirteen stripes, alternate red and white; that the union be thirteen stars, white in a blue field representing a new constellation." Elizabeth (Betsy) Ross made flags for the patriot forces, but in spite of legend, there is no proof that she made the first Stars and Stripes.

Howe believed that the war could only be won if he managed to destroy the main American army commanded by Washington. To destroy Washington's army, he first needed to force Washington to fight a battle. But Howe believed that Washington had 8,000 soldiers at Morristown. (In fact the American army was half that size.) Also, Howe knew that the American position at Morristown was difficult to attack because of the hilly land around it. So, Howe thought that the best way to make Washington fight was not to attack Morristown. Instead, he planned to march against the rebel capital at Philadelphia.

Howe thought about marching through New Jersey toward Philadelphia. If he did that, he would have to keep a supply line running 90 miles back to New York City. Meanwhile, Washington's army would be at Morristown in a position on Howe's flank. In war an enemy army that can attack a flank is very dangerous. Howe decided that guarding his supply against a flank attack by Washington was too risky. On April 2, 1777, Howe made a new plan. He would invade Pennsylvania by sea.

A loyalist who knew George Washington wrote, "He certainly deserves some merit as a general, that he, with his banditti [group of bandits] can keep General Howe dancing from one town to another for two years."

A Trap in New Jersey

During the late winter and early spring the American army at Morristown slowly grew stronger. Most of the new soldiers had no battle experience. Washington ordered many small raids against the British in New Jersey. He had three purposes: to harass the British, to give his men experience, and to build up the morale (spirits) of his army.

Because he knew that soon Howe would begin a new campaign, Washington moved his army from Morristown to Middle Brook. There it was in a better position to move

quickly to block the British if Howe marched against Philadelphia or up the Hudson River. Middle Brook was only about seven miles from a British base at Brunswick.

Howe thought that Washington's new position gave him a chance to fight the big battle that he wanted. Howe marched about 18,000 men into New Jersey on June 12. But Washington's position at Middle Brook was strong, so Howe refused to attack. Instead, Howe set a trap for Washington. He ordered his army to retreat quickly and act as though it was afraid to fight. Howe hoped that Washington would chase his army. When Washington did move down from the hills, Howe ordered his army to turn around. At 1 A.M. on June 26 the British army made a surprise night march to try to get between Washington and his escape route into the hills.

Howe's trap almost worked. But Washington saw the danger and managed to retreat quickly back into the hills. Howe had spent one month marching around New Jersey in an effort to force Washington to fight.

Besides trying to destroy Washington's army, British forces also raided important rebel supply bases. During an April 1777 raid against Danbury, Connecticut, the patriot General David Wooster received a mortal wound.

Washington again proved himself to be a good general. He was too careful and too clever to fall into Howe's trap. A discouraged British colonel concluded that the Americans "have too much caution to risk everything" in one battle.

In 1777, unlike in 1776, Howe was able to begin his campaign against Washington early in the spring. Because Howe failed to force Washington to fight a battle, Howe failed to take advantage of his early start.

People in America and in Europe began to see that Washington was doing something amazing: He was keeping his army alive against Great Britain's heaviest attacks. A loyalist wrote: "That a Negro-driver [Washington owned slaves] should, with a ragged [group] of undisciplined people, the scum and refuse of all nations on earth, so long keep a British general at bay, nay, even [make] him, with as fine an army of veteran soldiers as ever England had on the American continent, to retreat—it is astonishing."

CHAPTER TWO

The Philadelphia Campaign

At the end of 1776, when British soldiers reached the Delaware River, the Continental Congress had fled from Philadelphia to Baltimore. There it made some decisions that gave General Washington important extra powers. Washington was already the commander-in-chief of the American army, but Congress had made most military decisions. Washington's new powers allowed him to raise more regular, or Continental, soldiers, including a corps of engineers. Washington could appoint all officers under the rank of general for the new units. There was more.

Washington could call out the militia without having to ask permission from Congress. That would save time during an emergency. The commander-in-chief's power to call out the militia became one of the key powers of all future United States presidents. Washington's army was always short of supplies. Congress gave Washington the power "to take . . . whatever he may want" from civilians. Washington had to use continental money (the paper money that Congress printed) to pay for what he took. But everyone knew that the continental money was not worth very much. So Congress gave Washington the power to arrest anyone who refused to accept the paper money.

Rebel leaders understood that all of those decisions were dangerous. They believed that the American revolt against the British King George was a battle against tyranny (cruel, unjust rule). Now some rebel leaders worried that they had given Washington so much power that he too might become a tyrant.

Other rebel leaders were not worried. One wrote: "We have given General Washington large and ample powers. . . . Thus the Business of War will . . . move in

The waterfront at Philadelphia, where a Continental navy warship is being prepared for a mission.

Above: General John Burgoyne was busy with his campaign in the north while Howe turned his attention to Philadelphia.

Opposite Top: The French engineer officer, Louis le Begue de Presle Duportail worked on the Delaware River forts. These forts persuaded Lord Howe to avoid sailing up the river and cost the British valuable time.

Opposite Below: Lord Howe's fleet sails from Sandy Hook for Philadelphia.

the proper channels," and Congress would no longer try to control "matters of which it is supremely [completely] ignorant."

Some leaders believed that Congress was so afraid the rebels were about to lose the war that they had become desperate. One such leader wrote, "Congress have given up most of their Power to the Generals...if this don't save [Philadelphia] nothing we can do will."

Congress faced a difficult job. It had to figure out what was the right kind of government for America at the same time it was fighting a war for survival.

Howe Moves to Head of Elk

While Howe and Washington were marching around New Jersey in June and July of 1777, another British army commanded by General John Burgoyne was on the move (see Volume 5). Burgoyne planned to march south from Canada. His first goal was to capture Fort Ticonderoga. Then he planned to march to the Hudson River near Albany, New York. Once Burgoyne reached the Hudson River, he would be in a good position to cooperate with British forces in New York City.

For the British side it was vital that the different British forces cooperated. It was the job of the British government to make sure that the generals and admirals worked together. But it took a long time to communicate back and forth across the Atlantic Ocean. By the time everyone agreed what to do, something unexpected took place (like Washington's surprise attack at Trenton). Then, new plans had to be made. A British general complained, "...plans of war made in [London] at several thousand miles distant from the scene of action [America] are not always good."

Howe knew about Burgoyne's plans. But he decided to continue with his own plan to capture Philadelphia. In London the official in charge of the effort to crush the American rebellion, the Secretary of State for American Colonies George Germain, approved of Howe's strategy. He called it "solid and decisive." Howe left about 3,000 men in New York. Their job was to guard the city and to help Burgoyne if they could.

Between July 9 and July 11 about 14,000 British

soldiers loaded onto transport ships. Howe waited until July 16. On that day he received a message from Burgoyne that Burgoyne's invasion was going well. This information gave Howe the confidence to order his army to leave New York.

The Royal Navy controlled the sea. Its ships could go anywhere they wanted because the rebel navy was too small to stop them. The fact that the Royal Navy could safely carry the army anywhere along the American coast was a big advantage for Howe. Howe planned to use that advantage by having the navy take his army to the mouth of the Delaware River near Wilmington, Delaware. Then it could move up the river toward Philadelphia. But sailing ships cannot move unless the wind blows in the right direction. The wind was not right until July 23. Half the campaign season was over, and Howe had not even begun.

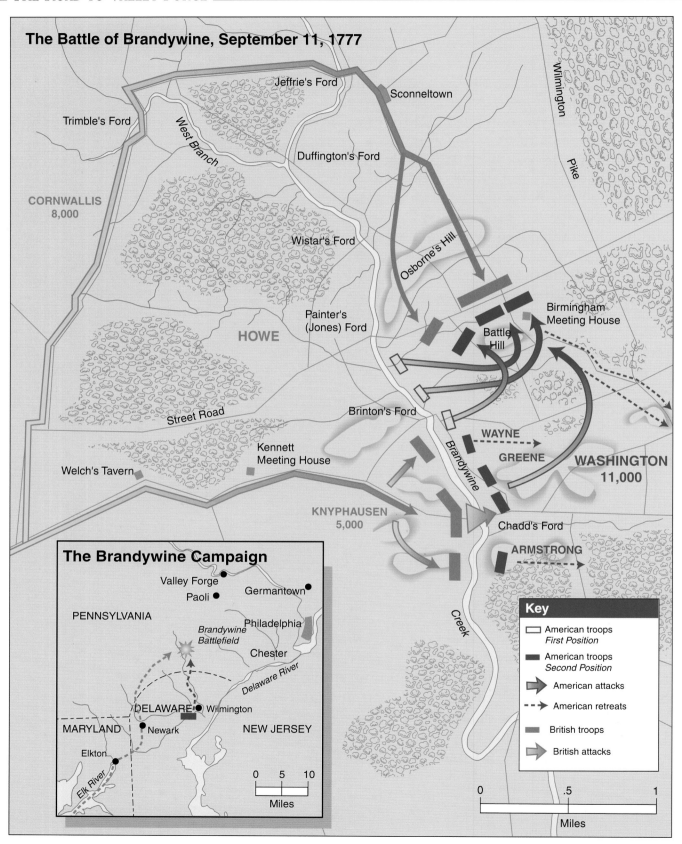

The Battle of Brandywine, September 11, 1777

Jeffrie's Ford

Sconneltown

Trimble's Ford

West Branch

Duffington's Ford

CORNWALLIS
8,000

Wistar's Ford

Osborne's Hill

Birmingham
Meeting House

HOWE

Painter's
(Jones) Ford

Battle
Hill

Brinton's Ford

Street Road

WAYNE

Brandywine

GREENE

WASHINGTON
11,000

Kennett
Meeting House

Welch's Tavern

KNYPHAUSEN
5,000

Chadd's Ford

ARMSTRONG

Creek

The Brandywine Campaign

Valley Forge

Paoli

Germantown

PENNSYLVANIA

*Brandywine
Battlefield*

Philadelphia

Chester

Delaware River

DELAWARE ● Wilmington

MARYLAND ● Newark

NEW JERSEY

Elkton

Elk River

0   5   10

Miles

Key

☐ American troops
First Position

■ American troops
Second Position

➡ American attacks

- - -➤ American retreats

▬ British troops

➡ British attacks

0   .5   1

Miles

More delays came when the fleet carrying Howe's army arrived at the mouth of the Delaware. There it met a British patrol ship. The captain of that ship told the commander of the British fleet, Lord Richard Howe (General Howe's brother), that it was too hard to sail up the Delaware River. He added that the rebels had built many forts to guard the river.

Lord Howe could have found out about the situation on the Delaware River weeks earlier. But he had never shown much interest in crushing the rebels. Because he was not really dedicated to winning the war, he failed to show energy and leadership. Given the information that the Delaware River was not a good route, Lord Howe decided to take his fleet to Chesapeake Bay.

Lord Howe's decision was a mistake. If he had continued up the Delaware, he certainly could have landed the army somewhere like New Castle, Delaware. Instead, Lord Howe ordered the fleet to sail to Chesapeake Bay. Finally, on August 25 the British army landed at Head of Elk (a small town at the head of the Elk River). By taking the fleet to Chesapeake Bay, Lord Howe wasted another 25 days. The British did not gain anything by that movement because Head of Elk was only 12 miles away from New Castle and no closer to Philadelphia.

Four companies of American militia guarded the place where the British landed. They ran away without firing a shot. So, the poor British soldiers finally walked again on dry land. They had been aboard the transports for 47 summer days. During that time they had suffered from heat, thirst, and lack of exercise. Many soldiers got sick. The voyage was even harder on the army's horses. A large number of the horses died during the voyage. Until the army replaced the horses, it could not move very far. So, Howe sent patrols to take horses from nearby farms and villages, further delaying the British advance to Philadelphia.

Meanwhile, George Washington marched his army to block Howe from capturing Philadelphia. August 24 was a fine summer day in Philadelphia. The city people gathered to watch the army march out of the city. In the lead rode the commander-in-chief, carefully dressed in a

Henry Knox taught himself about how to use artillery in war. In contrast, British artillery specialists received formal training from experienced military men.

The Foreign Volunteers

In 1777 many foreign officers came to America to join the rebel side. Many came simply for the adventure, to earn a reputation in a war, or to make money. Many of them spoke very little English and had no interest in learning how to get along with the common American soldiers. Very few were willing to accept any but the highest ranks.

Still, many of these volunteers impressed Congress. Congress appointed some to high command. This angered Washington's three most important generals, John Sullivan, Henry Knox, and Nathanael Greene. They had served loyally and risked their lives for more than a year. It seemed unfair to them that some foreigner should suddenly appear and become a general at an equal or higher rank. They told Congress that they would resign if Congress appointed foreign generals.

An American diplomat in Paris, Silas Deane (on right), accepted European volunteers (Lafayette on left, de Kalb in center) who wanted to fight for the rebels in America.

Congress saw this complaint as a deadly threat to Congress's authority (the power to make decisions). Congress refused to be "controlled" by its generals. It debated whether to dismiss the three generals or even to arrest them. Finally, Congress decided to demand an apology.

Until this time John Adams and Nathanael Greene had been close friends. Both men were devoted to the American cause. Adams tried to explain to Greene that this issue was about the need "of preserving the Authority of the Civil Powers [Congress] over the military." If Congress backed down, one thing would lead to another "until the Officers of the Army will do as most others have done, [take] all Authority out of civil Hands and set up a Tyrant of their own." Greene disagreed, and this feud ended their friendship.

As time passed, American leaders began to see which foreign officers were qualified and which were not. The qualified men received important assignments. They included the Frenchman Louis Duportail and the Pole Thaddeus Kosciuszko. These officers greatly improved the Continental Army's engineering. Another Pole, Casimir Pulaski, organized the army's first good cavalry unit. The German Johann de Kalb proved to be a brave combat leader. Friedrich von Steuben, another German, became an excellent trainer for the infantry.

The 19-year-old Marquis de Lafayette, a French nobleman, was exceptional. Unlike the other foreign volunteers, he asked for neither a command nor pay. He said, "After the sacrifices I have made [in order to come to America], I have the right to expect two favours; one is to serve at my own expense, the other is to serve, at first, as volunteer." George Washington took a special liking to Lafayette, and the two men became very close friends.

Left: The Pole Casimir Pulaski brought his knowledge about cavalry to America to help the rebels.

Below: Lafayette quickly became close to Washington. Washington loved him like a son.

blue uniform with buff facings (facings are the trim color for a uniform and usually appeared on the collar, cuff, and turnbacks, or inside of the jacket). Three officers who served as Washington's aides rode next to Washington. They were the artillery officer Henry Knox, the military secretary Tench Tilghman, and a young French nobleman who had volunteered to help the rebel cause, the Marquis de Lafayette.

The main strength of the army, the infantry, or foot soldiers, followed Washington. An experienced American officer watched the army march by. He saw that it looked much better than it ever had before. He wrote, "Though [poorly] dressed" (the soldiers did not have regular uniforms and many wore civilian clothes) they "held well [polished] arms and carried them like soldiers." This officer thought that the army had a good chance to beat the British.

After the British landed at Head of Elk, Washington still did not want to risk his army in a battle. But it is the business of an army to fight. Washington knew that. Congress, many patriots everywhere, and even the army itself expected him to fight to save Philadelphia. So, Washington led the army toward Wilmington, Delaware, a town near where the British had landed.

On August 28 Howe ordered his army to begin a march north toward Philadelphia. The British had not yet recovered from the sea voyage. So, Howe's men marched slowly. Because he did not have good cavalry who could scout for him, Washington was unsure exactly where the British army was. Finally, on September 9 Washington shifted his army from the Wilmington area to a position along Brandywine Creek. Two days later, on September 11, 1777, Howe's army attacked.

The Battle of Brandywine

Unlike Washington, Howe knew very well where his enemy was located. Howe knew that the rebel army was seven miles away in a position behind Brandywine Creek. The creek was not a very good defensive position because it had many crossing places, or fords. Still, Howe decided against making a direct attack across the

creek. Instead, he sent 5,000 men commanded by the German General Wilhelm Knyphausen to make a feint, or fake attack, at Chadd's Ford. Howe ordered General Charles Cornwallis to take the rest of the army, about 7,500 men, around Washington's right flank. This was the same sort of plan that had worked so well on Long Island one year earlier. Howe hoped that it would work again in Pennsylvania.

George Washington shows the Stars and Stripes to Lafayette and to a unit of American continentals. In fact, the stars on the flag were not arranged in a circle until the 1790s.

General William Alexander claimed that he held the British title "Lord Stirling," although he did not. Still, the Americans called him "Lord Stirling." He proved a good combat leader.

Compared to British generals, rebel generals such as Nathanael Greene were inexperienced.

The American army numbered about 11,000 men. Washington expected an attack at Chadd's Ford. There he placed his best troops, a division commanded by Nathanael Greene and a brigade commanded by Anthony Wayne. Most of the American artillery was there as well. About 800 light infantry crossed the ford to the west side. Their job was to detect any enemy forces who advanced against Chadd's Ford. General John Armstrong's Pennsylvania militia guarded Washington's left flank. Hilly ground there made any British attack difficult. That is why Washington used his worst soldiers, the militia, to defend the position.

Washington knew that there were many fords upstream of Chadd's Ford. He ordered General Sullivan's division to defend those fords. Washington also sent all of his cavalry to the west side of the creek to look for any British attack against Sullivan's position. Washington kept two more divisions, commanded by General Alexander (also known as Stirling) and General Adam Stephen, in reserve, or behind the front line. Washington planned to use the reserves once he knew where the British were.

The British outnumbered the Americans 13,000 to 11,000. This was not a very big British advantage, especially since the Americans had the advantage of being in a defensive position. But the British officers and men were much more experienced in war. For example, the German General Knyphausen, who was to march against Chadd's Ford, had joined the Prussian Army in 1734. He had 43 years of military experience. The rebel General Greene, who commanded the Americans defending Chadd's Ford, had joined the militia in 1773. His real military experience began in November 1776 during the fighting around New York City. Greene had less than one year of military experience.

It was the same story with the professional British and Hessian soldiers compared to the American Continentals. Most of the British and Hessians had trained together for years. Most of the American

Continentals first joined the army in the spring of 1777. The American militia had only recently joined the army. When soldiers fight a battle, they become surrounded by noise, confusion, and fear. At such times training and discipline hold a unit together. At the Battle of Brandywine the British were completely trained and disciplined. The Americans had only a little training and discipline.

The two British columns commanded by Cornwallis and Knyphausen left camp at dawn on September 11. Knyphausen's column met Maxwell's light infantry around 8 A.M. William Maxwell told Washington what was happening and moved his light infantry back across Brandywine Creek to join the main army. By 10:30 Knyphausen was in position at Chadd's Ford.

Since Knyphausen did not attack the ford, Washington and his generals guessed that Howe was making his main attack somewhere else. Then, around 11 A.M. Washington received reports that Cornwallis's column was moving against his right flank. Washington ordered his cavalry to scout for Cornwallis in order to make certain that the reports were true. Next, Washington received a message from General Sullivan, the officer whose job it was to defend the American right flank. Sullivan said that some militia had been on the roads where Cornwallis was supposed to be. The militia said that they had not seen any British soldiers. Sullivan concluded that the earlier reports "must be wrong."

Washington was uncertain what to do. He decided to wait for more information. Early in the afternoon a farmer rode to Washington's headquarters and demanded to see the general. The farmer told Washington that the British were about to surround his army! Washington did not believe it was possible. But at 2 P.M. his cavalry sent a report that the British had crossed Brandywine Creek and were only two miles from Sullivan's men.

Above: An American soldier calmly pours gunpowder into his musket as he reloads during a battle. It was very hard to remain calm during the terror and excitement of battle.

Right: A British grenadier, one of the elite soldiers in the British army. The British regulars had years of training so they could remain steady during a battle.

The Hessians

The British hired about 30,000 German soldiers to help their army put down the rebellion in America. Several of the commanders and units of hired soldiers came from the two German states of Hesse-Cassel and Hesse-Hanau. So the German soldiers all came to be called "Hessians."

To hire the Hessians, England made treaties with the princes of six German states. They agreed to pay the German soldiers the same wage they paid to British soldiers. In addition, they agreed to pay a fee to the princes for each soldier. Therefore, the German princes wanted to send as many men as possible to America. They ordered German officers to round up thousands of men and force them to join the army. Once the men joined the army, they received the strict German training that made them ready for war.

At the beginning of the Revolutionary War the British respected the well-trained and disciplined Hessian soldiers. But the British soon came to dislike the Hessians because they were too different. Few of the Hessians spoke English, and British and Hessian soldiers had little to do with one another. A Hessian chaplain wrote a letter complaining of "the proud and insulting looks which the English . . . cast on the Germans."

The Americans feared the Hessians until they had defeated them at Trenton and Bennington. They soon realized that hired soldiers might not be devoted to the British cause. Many Hessians, in turn, came to see America as a place where they could have better lives. About 5,000 of them deserted their army to stay in America. Some of them slipped away into the Pennsylvania countryside, where they could blend in with the German-speaking population.

German recruiters drag away a husband and father so he can serve as a mercenary in the war against the American rebels.

A soldier in the loyalist unit, the Queen's Rangers

The situation was dangerous, but Washington believed that he could deal with it. He ordered Sullivan to fight the British and sent the reserves commanded by Alexander and Stephen to help Sullivan. Now the inexperience of the Americans caused problems. The various rebel units had trouble getting in the right positions to fight effectively against Cornwallis.

Cornwallis's men had done well to get around the American flank. They had marched about 17 miles in 11 hours with only about a one-hour break to rest and eat. An American civilian saw the British approach. He wrote, "In a few minutes the fields were . . . covered over with them [the British soldiers]. . . . Their arms and bayonets being raised, shone as bright as silver." General Cornwallis rode by. He "appeared tall, and sat very [straight]. His rich scarlet clothing loaded with gold lace."

At 4:30 the main battle began. The British attacked fiercely. For about 45 minutes the Americans stopped them. Meanwhile, back at Chadd's Ford, when Knyphausen heard the sounds of the fighting, he too attacked. A loyalist fighting in a unit called the Queen's Rangers was in the thick of the fighting at Chadd's Ford. He wrote that there was a rebel "battery playing upon us with grapeshot [large, round, iron balls] which did much execution. The water [of Brandywine Creek was] up to our breasts and was much stained with blood before the battery was [captured] and the guns turned upon the enemy." Slowly Knyphausen's men advanced through the American center.

Many of the Americans at the Battle of Brandywine had little battle experience. Yet enough stood their ground to make a hard fight.

Washington himself rode to the right and arrived about 5:30. He was just in time to see his men start to fall apart. He and his officers, including Lafayette, rode among the men, shouting to them to stand firm. Lafayette was hit in the thigh with a bullet. Many Continental units, particularly the artillery, fought well. But the best soldiers in the British army, the elite Foot Guards, made a charge that broke the American line.

One of Greene's units, Weedon's Brigade, arrived in time to cover the American retreat. The fighting ended around 7 P.M. Most of the rebel soldiers did not run away but instead retreated in good order. Still, Washington was unable to reorganize his army until about midnight.

At the Battle of Brandywine the Americans lost about 1,250 men, 400 of whom were prisoners. The British also captured 11 rebel artillery pieces. The British lost 577 killed and wounded. Only six British soldiers were reported missing, a low number that showed that Howe's army was very well disciplined.

There was no doubt that Brandywine was an American defeat. Both sides had fought bravely, but General Howe and his officers had done better than Washington and his officers. Washington had been slow to make up his mind what to do. Washington's biographer later wrote that Washington fought the battle "as if he had been in a daze." It was especially embarrassing for Washington that Howe had beat him in just the same way as at the Battle of Long Island.

Still, even though Howe had won the battle, he did not manage to destroy Washington's army. A historian later wrote that Washington's army "had been as badly beaten as any army could be without being entirely destroyed." But the army had not panicked. Washington and most of his men lived to fight another day.

The Rhode Island Regiment carried this flag at the battle. The flag showed thirteen stars to represent the thirteen states and had the word "Hope" above an anchor. The anchor symbolized the state's seafaring tradition.

The courageous Lafayette received a wound at the Battle of Brandywine.

CHAPTER THREE

The British Capture Philadelphia

The discouraging defeat at the Battle of Brandywine depressed all patriots, including John Adams.

After the Battle of Brandywine Washington rallied his army. He moved it to get between Howe and Philadelphia. Meanwhile, Howe rested his army. Messengers carried the news of Washington's defeat to Philadelphia. They woke congressmen up to attend an emergency 6 A.M. meeting on September 13.

Congress realized that the British were likely to capture the capital. So, it decided to remove all important military supplies from Philadelphia to Reading, 50 miles away. At the same time, people made frantic efforts to remove books and papers from the State Library, money and papers from the Public Loan Office, and all court documents. Authorities ordered that all bells, including the Liberty Bell, be taken down and sent off to safety. Congress also called for reinforcements, including Continentals from New York and the militia from Maryland, New Jersey, and Virginia. Finally, Congress prepared to move itself once again to escape from the British.

The notion that the British were about to capture America's biggest city annoyed many congressmen. They blamed Washington for the defeat at Brandywine. Even one of Washington's supporters, John Adams, had doubts. Adams wrote a prayer in his diary:

"Oh Heaven! grant us one great Soul! One leading Mind would [save] the best Cause [the rebel cause] from the Ruin which seems to await it. . . . We have as good a Cause, as ever was fought for. We have great Resources. The People are well [ready]. One active masterly [leader] would bring order out of this Confusion and save this County."

Six days later, on September 16, Howe marched toward Philadelphia. It seemed likely that another major battle would take place at Warren Tavern. Instead, a hard rain began to fall. A Hessian officer wrote, "I wish I could give a description of the downpour which began during the engagement and continued until the next morning. It came down so hard that in a few moments we were drenched and sank in mud up to our calves."

Soldiers in the Revolutionary War carried their ammunition in leather boxes called cartridge boxes. Cartridge boxes were supposed to be waterproof. The cartridge boxes carried by the British and Hessian soldiers on that day kept their ammunition dry. But the American cartridge boxes failed. So much ammunition got wet that entire rebel regiments were unable to fire a shot. For that reason Washington decided to avoid a battle.

During the next days Howe skillfully moved his army. Time and again Washington saw that he had no choice but to retreat. His army suffered during this time. The fall weather was wet and cold. The rebels had neither blankets nor tents. At least 1,000 men had no shoes. The supply system broke down, and most men went hungry. Then came another small disaster.

The Paoli Massacre

Thirty-two-year-old Anthony Wayne was the son of a prosperous Pennsylvania tanner. Before the war he had won election to the Pennsylvania legislature and served on the committee of safety. Even though he had no military experience, he became colonel of a Pennsylvania unit on January 3, 1776. Wayne led the unit during the American invasion of Canada. He received a promotion to brigadier general in the spring of 1777. He joined Washington's army and commanded the Pennsylvania Continentals. At all times Wayne showed great bravery and energy. As he gained

A well-made cartridge box with a long enough cover to keep the rain out.

experience, he became an excellent soldier.

Because he knew the area well, Wayne received orders to harass Howe's advance against Philadelphia. Wayne moved his division with 1,500 men and four guns to a secret position near Paoli Tavern, about 15 miles west of Philadelphia. He planned to make a surprise attack against the British flank. But the British learned about his plan and also learned where he had camped.

A British general, Charles Grey, left the British camp on the night of September 20. Grey planned to surprise Wayne's men while they were still in the camp. Fighting at night is difficult because it is very hard for leaders to control the movements of their men. It is also hard to tell friends from enemies. Grey gave special orders to his men. A British officer, Major John André, wrote, "No soldier...was suffered to load [his musket]; those who could not [unload] their pieces took out the flints." Without the flints the soldiers could not shoot. In this way the British knew that anyone who fired was an enemy.

The British silently advanced to Wayne's camp well before dawn on September 21. Four American guards saw them and fired warning shots. The Pennsylvania soldiers rose from their sleep and tried to form for battle. The British charged. Because their muskets were unloaded, the British used their bayonets to stab the rebels. A short, bloody battle took place. But the surprise British attack was too much for Wayne's men. They fled from the camp.

The Americans lost about 150 men killed, wounded, and captured. The British lost only 6 killed and 22 wounded. After the battle local citizens found 53 bodies that showed terrible wounds. British bayonets had

Anthony Wayne was a fine combat commander, but he allowed his men to be victims of a surprise attack at Paoli.

caused the wounds. American writers used that fact to make the claim that Grey's soldiers had refused to let rebel soldiers surrender. By making that claim, the writers tried to increase American hatred of the British.

However, during the fight the British captured 71 men and took them back to their own camp. The British also left about 40 rebel wounded in nearby houses. Although history remembered the fight as the "Paoli Massacre," in fact there had not been any massacre.

Grey received much credit for his skillful leadership. He earned the nickname "No-flint." Wayne was greatly embarrassed by the battle. He demanded a court martial (a military trial) to examine his behavior. The court voted that Wayne had acted "with the highest honors" and was not guilty of anything wrong.

The most important result of the combat at Paoli was that it discouraged Washington's army. The thought that they were not safe even while in their own camps struck fear into the rebel soldiers. Added to that fear was the fact that during the 11 days after the Battle of Brandywine, Washington's army marched 140 miles. The men suffered from terrible weather. Sickness and desertion reduced the army by half.

Meanwhile, Howe continued with his skillful maneuvers. As he came nearer to Philadelphia, people in the city grew anxious. The rumor that Howe was about to enter the city caused a 1 A.M. alarm. Men went door to door to wake everyone up. People immediately began to flee the city. A woman described the scene: "... wagons rattling, horses galloping, women running,

British soldiers stab and kill American soldiers around their campfires at Paoli on September 21, 1777.

children crying, [congressional] delegates flying, & altogether the greatest [confusion] fright & terror that can be imagined."

The president of the Continental Congress, South Carolinian Henry Laurens, saw that even some congressmen were in a panic. He wrote, "Fright sometimes works Lunacy. This does not imply that Congress is frightened or Lunatic but there may be some men [fleeing the city] who may be much of one and a little of the other."

On September 26 the British marched into Philadelphia. First to enter the city were the cavalry and two Philadelphia loyalists. Then came a military band playing "God Save the King."

The loyalists greeted the British as liberators. A loyalist newspaper reported that "A perfect tranquility [peacefulness] now prevails in the city. Numbers [of loyalists] who have been obliged to hide themselves from the former tyranny [the rebel government] . . . have appeared . . . to welcome the dawn of returning liberty."

An Ugly Side of the Rebellion

No one knows how many Americans supported the rebellion and how many stayed loyal to Great Britain. It is estimated that about one-third were rebels, one-third loyalists, and one-third neutral, but this is just a guess. During the war everyone knew that Philadelphia and the area around the city had many loyalists. There were also many Quakers, people whose religion taught them that fighting in any war was wrong. When Howe's army approached Philadelphia, Congress worried about the loyalists and Quakers. Congress feared that some of them would act as spies for Howe. On August 25, 1777, Congress passed a resolution that people in Pennsylvania and Delaware who were known to be against the war be put in jail.

Henry Laurens, the president of the Continental Congress at the time Congress evacuated Philadelphia

The Battle of Germantown

The British capture of the largest American city did not discourage most rebels. It did have an effect on Europe. European leaders did not understand how the war in America was very different from war in Europe. At that time, if a European country lost its largest city and capital to an enemy force, it was a disaster. European leaders figured that the American loss of Philadelphia might mean that total British victory was near. French leaders in particular again wondered if the American rebellion was just about over. Then came news of another dramatic battle at a place called Germantown.

When Howe captured Philadelphia, his work was not quite done. The rebels still held some forts downstream from Philadelphia. Those forts stopped British ships from sailing up the Delaware River to the city. Howe and his army needed to capture the forts so their ships could bring supplies to Philadelphia.

Howe divided his forces. He sent a powerful group to attack the forts. Cornwallis stayed in Philadelphia with

Forty-one citizens of Philadelphia were collected for questioning. Authorities said that as long as they promised not to help the British, and as long as they stayed in their homes (house arrest), they would not have to go to prison. Nineteen men agreed. The others were locked up. The prisoners demanded that Congress explain why they were in jail. Congress ignored them. Two more prisoners agreed to accept house arrest.

Congress sent the rest of them to prison in Virginia. During the winter of 1777–78 the prisoners and their families sent many petitions to Congress asking that they be allowed to live like other citizens. The prisoners pointed out that there was no proof that they had done anything illegal. Finally, in April 1778 Congress released the prisoners. Two had died during the time they were held prisoner.

When the survivors returned to Philadelphia, they again asked Congress to explain why they had been arrested. Again they received no answer. Congress had made a mistake, but it was too ashamed to admit it.

a second force to protect the city. Howe moved the rest of his army, about 9,000 men, five miles north of Philadelphia to a small village called Germantown. Because they believed that the rebels were too badly damaged from the Battle of Brandywine, the British did not expect to fight another battle against Washington any time soon.

Washington had shown in the past that he was an aggressive general. He had made surprise attacks at Trenton and Princeton. When Washington learned that Howe had split his army, he decided to attack again. After Brandywine Congress had ordered reinforcements for Washington. Washington's army had gained strength and numbered about 8,000 Continentals and 3,000 militia.

The Americans' first line of defense for the Delaware River was at Billingsport, New Jersey. When the British attacked, Continental marines helped evacuate the position in October 1777.

A private in a 1777 Pennsylvania State Regiment. The state troops were between militia and Continentals; they served longer than militia but not as long as Continentals.

Washington's strategy to make a surprise attack was good. The way he planned the attack was poor. He ordered four large groups to march sixteen miles along different roads toward Germantown. The columns began the march at 7 P.M. on October 3. Washington's plan required all the columns to be in a position to attack before dawn on October 4. The reason his plan was poor was that it was based on the expectation that everything would go smoothly. In war things never go smoothly, and Washington should have realized this.

The first problems began during the night march. Many Americans were barefoot. The roads were rough.

So, the men did not march as fast as Washington expected. A guide leading the biggest rebel column got lost, so that column was especially late. Before dawn a thick fog covered the ground. Men could barely see 30 yards. The American columns did not know where the other columns were located. When the battle began, each column had to fight its own battle without help from nearby friendly forces.

Above: During the Battle of Germantown Wayne's Pennsylvania men met the same British Light Infantry that had attacked them at Paoli. Wayne reported that "the rage and fury of the soldiers were not to be restrained for some time." His men savagely bayoneted British soldiers who were trying to surrender and wounded British soldiers.

The Americans attacked bravely. In most places the surprised British put up a tough defense. Still, the rebels pushed the British back. An American soldier wrote: "The enemy were driven quite through their camp. They left their kettles, in which they were cooking their breakfasts, on the fires....Affairs went on well for some time. The enemy were retreating before us."

But the leading rebel division ran out of ammunition. That gave the British a chance to rally. Then an accident took place. Because of the fog an American unit blundered into the rear of Wayne's division. The unit

A small British force took shelter inside the Chew House. The Americans tried unsuccessfully to drive them from the house.

thought that Wayne's men were British and opened fire. Their mistake caused a panic: "...the men came back on the run, some frantic with fear, some able to gasp a few words — that the enemy was in the rear, that the flank had been turned, that friends had been mistaken for foes, that orders to retreat had been shouted."

Washington and his officers tried desperately to rally the men. They failed. By 10 A.M. the battle was over, with the American army running for safety. Washington's army lost 152 killed, 521 wounded, and more than 400 captured. British losses were about half as many: 537 killed and wounded and 14 captured.

The defeat discouraged Washington. He believed that his army had been about to win a great victory when the accident took place and the army panicked. He concluded his battle report by writing, "In a word, it was a bloody day. Would to heaven I could add that it had been a more fortunate one for us."

Even though the Battle of Germantown was another defeat, it encouraged Washington's men. They had seen

Rebel soldiers shoot at the British defenders of the Chew House.

the enemy retreating, and that gave them hope. They shared Washington's belief that they had almost won. An American officer wrote that after the battle the soldiers "are in high spirits and appear to wish...for another engagement."

Germantown also had an important effect on French attitudes. The news of the great rebel victory at Saratoga had already reached Paris. Because of Saratoga the French government had decided to support the American rebels. But French leaders were uncertain if the rebels were going to be reliable allies. French leaders worried that the rebellion might collapse, and then France would be left to fight Britain by itself. The fact that the rebels lost their capital but still managed to attack the British at Germantown greatly encouraged the French. France decided to send powerful forces to help the rebels.

French help could not arrive until the spring of 1778. Before that help came, Washington and his army had to carry on the fight alone.

The Conway Cabal

After his victory at Germantown General Howe continued with the campaign to capture the American forts blocking the Delaware River. The two main American forts were named Fort Mifflin, on the Pennsylvania side of the river, and Fort Mercer on the New Jersey side. They were about seven miles downstream from Philadelphia. The Americans placed three lines of wooden stakes in the river to stop any British ships from moving past the forts.

British heavy artillery (siege guns) opened fire against one fort, Fort Mifflin, on October 10. Twelve days later, on October 22, a powerful Hessian force attacked Fort Mercer. Although the

A piece of the timber stockade sheathed with iron that blocked the Delaware River

Hessians attacked bravely, the rebels drove them back with heavy losses. Four hundred Hessians fell in the battle. The next day, October 23, warships belonging to the Royal Navy attacked. The Americans defeated that attack also and even managed to sink two British ships.

But the British kept adding forces to the attack. During the night of November 15–16 the rebels abandoned Fort Mifflin. Five nights later they abandoned Fort Mercer. The Delaware River was now open to British ships all the way to Philadelphia. Ever since the British had captured the city, the people of Philadelphia had faced a food shortage. After clearing the river, ships soon brought supplies for both the army and the civilians.

During the autumn of 1777 Washington tried hard to help the rebel forces defending the forts, but he failed to accomplish very much. Because of his loss of Philadelphia some army officers and congressmen criticized Washington's leadership.

Between the time Congress left Philadelphia and met again, major changes had been made among the delegates. Only six delegates among the 20 congressmen who had elected Washington to general in chief returned. Some who had elected Washington had died, others had resigned, and others had simply left to return

The British warship *Augusta* on fire off Fort Mifflin on October 23, 1777. The American fort is on the left.

British warships fight against the American forts guarding the Delaware River.

home. So, at the next meeting of Congress in York, Pennsylvania, very few of the delegates knew Washington personally.

The delegates compared Washington with General Horatio Gates, the victor at Saratoga (see Volume 5). Gates had won a stunning victory and forced the British General John Burgoyne's army to surrender. A critic of Washington wrote John Adams to praise Gates and note that Washington had been "outgeneraled and twice beaten" and forced to abandon Philadelphia. The critic was one of many who concluded that Congress should make a change and replace Washington.

Then a troublemaker named Thomas Conway got involved. Conway was born in Ireland. He went to France to be educated and served in the French army. In 1776 he came to America, and Congress made him a general. Conway did well in the army, but he badly wanted to be promoted. While trying to get promoted, he joined the group that was critical of Washington.

The leaders of the anti-Washington group were Samuel Adams, Richard Henry Lee, Thomas Mifflin, and Benjamin Rush. These patriots worried that Washington had too much power. They feared that he would become a tyrant. So, they took steps in Congress to limit Washington's power. One of the things Congress did was to promote Conway and name him Inspector General.

Benjamin Rush was one of the signers of the Declaration of Independence. On January 12, 1778, he wrote to Patrick Henry to recommend that General Washington be replaced.

The Inspector General had the duty of inspecting the army and then reporting to Congress. In a way, Conway was a spy for Congress whose job was to make sure that Washington was following orders from Congress.

Conway wrote letters criticizing Washington and claiming that he was only repeating what other officers had said. His letters also complained falsely to Congress that Washington was not cooperating with his inspections. Members of Congress finally saw through him. But Conway and other officers and politicians who criticized Washington did have some influence. Their efforts persuaded some people, including Washington himself, that an organized plot existed to remove him. The entire affair became known as the Conway Cabal (a cabal is a small group who work together for a secret purpose), though Conway played only a small part in the campaign of criticism.

In the years after the war all the way up to modern times historians have argued about the Conway Cabal. Most have concluded that it did not come close to overthrowing Washington. In fact, modern historians doubt that a very large or organized group existed that wanted to replace Washington. But what is important is what Washington believed. Washington thought that the Conway Cabal was real. He believed that his enemies were plotting to remove him from command just at the time that he and his army most needed help from Congress. Indeed, Congress, under the influence of Washington's critics, did not help Washington and his army as much as they could have during the winter at Valley Forge.

CHAPTER FIVE

Winter at Valley Forge

During the week before Christmas 1777 the rebel army went into winter quarters at Valley Forge, Pennsylvania. Valley Forge was about 20 miles from Philadelphia. The terrain was good for defense in case Howe attacked. It was close to a small river that provided water for drinking and cooking. A thick forest surrounded the camp, so the soldiers could find fuel for their fires and wood to build huts.

But the winter at Valley Forge was a time of terrible hardship. The American supply system broke down completely. By the middle of January 1778 nearly 4,000

Replicas of the huts used by soldiers at Valley Forge

George Washington leads the army to winter quarters at Valley Forge.

The inside of one of the huts used as winter quarters, showing sleeping platforms on the right.

In the lower left, a patrol struggles back to camp at Valley Forge.

men could not leave their huts because they did not have enough clothes to endure the cold. Soldiers often went very hungry because there was no food.

At one point Washington planned a raid. He had to cancel it because the soldiers could not leave their huts. They did not have shoes and clothing for a winter march. They did not have food to take with them during the march. The officer in charge of getting food for the army reported that he had no cattle to slaughter for meat. There were only 25 barrels of flour to feed the entire army.

At another point more than 3,000 men were unfit for duty. Many were sick. One soldier wrote, "I am sick—discontented—and out of humour. Poor food—hard lodgings—fatigue—nasty clothes—nasty cookery—vomit half my time . . . why are we sent here to starve and Freeze." During the six months the army lived at Valley Forge, about 2,500 men died. This total amounted to one man in four.

After the Revolutionary War Valley Forge became a national shrine to patriot suffering. Yet the winter of 1777–78 was actually a mild one. The soldiers suffered so much that winter for several reasons. The army's

supply service, the **Quartermaster**'s Department, was badly run. Many civilians had lost interest in the patriot cause. They did not make an effort to help the army. And many politicians, army officers, and civilians took advantage of the situation to make money.

For example, American businessmen hired hundreds of government wagons to carry food and supplies north from Pennsylvania. They made money selling the food and supplies. At the same time, a large supply of pork in New Jersey needed to be hauled to the army at Valley Forge. Because the wagons had all been hired out, the pork spoiled. Closer to Valley Forge local farmers sold food to the British in Philadelphia because the British paid using good money. If they sold to the rebel army, they were paid in nearly useless rebel paper money.

quartermaster: officer responsible for supplying an army with quarters (living space), clothing, and equipment. The Continental Army had a separate department for supplying food.

George Washington at Valley Forge

Meanwhile, many in Congress blamed Washington. One congressman said that Washington had been guilty of "such blunders as might have disgraced a soldier of three months standing." When Washington asked Congress to reform the Quartermaster's Department (the men in charge of supplying the army with everything except food), Congress ignored him. Washington reported to Congress that unless there was a quick change, his army would do one of three things: "Starve, dissolve, or disperse." Washington's reputation was so low at this time that most congressmen did not believe him.

In spite of the suffering, the army did not mutiny (a military revolt by the soldiers against their leaders). The number one reason they stayed loyal was that they had faith in George Washington.

51

Washington meets with a congressional committee at Valley Forge to try to show them how much the army is suffering.

Washington worked hard to improve conditions for his army. His devotion to the Revolution, and the Continental soldiers' devotion to their general in chief, convinced most of Congress that George Washington was still the right man to lead the Continental Army. Finally, his critics in Congress (including the men involved with the Conway Cabal) lost influence. Washington received permission from Congress to make reforms. He put the talented Nathanael Greene in charge of the Quartermaster's Department. He sent

Above Right: Friedrich Wilhelm von Steuben learned about war while serving in the Prussian army in Europe.

small groups of soldiers to nearby homes and farms to seize food and clothing. This did not make him popular with the people who had to surrender goods to the soldiers, but it did keep his soldiers alive.

Washington also sent some of his best soldiers and best leaders on long-range missions to gather supplies. Anthony Wayne led one mission into New Jersey. Captain Henry Lee, a 21-year-old Virginia officer (and the man who would become the father of Civil War General Robert E. Lee), led a cavalry force into Delaware. Meanwhile, at Valley Forge the German soldier Baron Friedrich Wilhelm von Steuben took charge of training the Continental soldiers.

At the age of 17 Steuben had begun serving as a staff officer in the Prussian Army (staff officers help generals organize and run an army). At that time the Prussian staff was the most modern in the world. Steuben brought his knowledge about organizing an army to Valley Forge on February 23, 1778. Steuben worked with Greene and Alexander Hamilton to create a training program for the soldiers. The program was a more simple version of the drill formations and movements used by European armies.

Steuben started with 100 men who were chosen because they were good soldiers. Even though he spoke no English, Steuben had a way of inspiring soldiers. He wore a magnificent uniform. He acted in such an entertaining way that men could not help but pay attention to him. He stood in front of the shivering soldiers, a translator at his side, and began with basic instruction. After his men learned basic drill like how to load and fire their weapons properly, he taught them more complicated lessons. Once the 100 chosen men proved that they had learned enough, Steuben sent them out to become teachers themselves. Every day, after working with the common soldiers, Steuben held special classes for the officers. He taught the officers how to give the correct orders so that the soldiers moved as a unit. In that way Steuben spread his knowledge throughout the American army.

Steuben also understood that American soldiers had to be told why something was important before they would

Washington stands in the snow looking over the huts at Valley Forge.

try to learn. Still, Steuben was quick to lose his temper when the men made mistakes. He would swear at the men in German and French. He realized that the soldiers did not understand him, so he called for an aide to swear for him in English. An eyewitness reported that Steuben's methods worked. When Steuben began swearing: "...a good-natured smile went through the ranks and at last the maneuver was properly performed."

Steuben's influence on the American army was huge. One historian has called Steuben's training program "the most remarkable achievement in rapid military training in the history of the world." By the time the army left Valley Forge, it had learned discipline and

Von Steuben inspects a shivering line of Continental soldiers during a snowstorm at Valley Forge.

respect for authority. The Continentals had become professional soldiers, able to meet the British on equal terms.

The British in Philadelphia

While Washington's army was at Valley Forge, Howe's army made its winter quarters in Philadelphia. For the

George Washington and his wife, Martha, talk with the soldiers on Christmas Day, 1777. Martha Washington was one of the few women with the army during its time at Valley Forge.

people of Philadelphia, having to put up with 11,000 British and Hessian soldiers made for trying times. Simply finding places to house so many soldiers was difficult. Most British officers, from General Howe down to the youngest ensign (the lowest officer rank), wanted to treat civilians fairly. For example, when a lady complained about her house being used by General

Cornwallis as his headquarters, Cornwallis immediately moved elsewhere.

The privates (lowest rank) behaved very differently. Many of the British and German soldiers had been

An American drawing called "British Heroism" shows British soldiers using their bayonets to herd stolen cattle.

recruited from the lowest classes. Many soldiers had joined the army rather than stay in prison. Those men took advantage of the civilians whenever they could. Within days of the army's arrival soldiers destroyed the fences in and around the city. They used the fence rails as firewood and to build huts and fortifications. Many Philadelphia rebels had left the city when the British came. The British and Hessian soldiers looted their empty homes. They also committed worse crimes, including rape and robbery.

There was so much crime that citizens were afraid to go out at night. To try to stop criminal behavior, Howe offered a large reward for information about who committed the crimes. The officers held courts-martial (military trials) almost every day and handed out severe sentences. If judged guilty, soldiers faced flogging with a whip. Sentences of 400 to 1,000 lashes (one lash counted as one blow with the whip) were common. For especially serious crimes soldiers received the death sentence. In spite of the punishment the crime continued.

Captain Allan McLane used his own money to equip a small unit of cavalry. During the winter his men earned the nickname "market stoppers" because they stopped Americans from taking their goods to Philadelphia to sell at the market to the British.

In normal times Philadelphia depended on farmers bringing their produce to market in the city. American militia surrounded Philadelphia and tried to stop this traffic. Prices for all goods rose dramatically. The high prices provided an opportunity for some people to get rich. They brought scarce goods such as beef, cheese, flour, or rum into the city and sold the goods at a tremendous profit. In wartime such behavior is called profiteering. British and loyalist officials as well as British and Hessian officers took part in profiteering. One merchant wrote, "If we must suffer misfortunes [the troubles caused by the soldiers] we ought to drain all the [money] from them possible."

General Howe had named a Philadelphia loyalist, Joseph Galloway, to run Philadelphia. Galloway tried to end profiteering. On January 22, 1778, he made a law that stopped people from buying goods for resale at any place except the public market. Galloway's idea was that officials could watch the sales of goods in the market and control profiteering. Corrupt officials, including army officers, found ways to get around Galloway's law.

The rich people in Philadelphia could afford to buy what they needed. Stores near the river sold wines, sugar, soap, butter, silk, paper, combs, razors, and all sorts of other goods. A female merchant advertised in the *Pennsylvania Evening Post* on February 24, 1778, that her store had such luxuries as pickled walnuts, cucumbers, perfume, and peppers for sale. Robert Bell's book store did a good business among the British officers.

Everyone who was not rich suffered. Many people had to sell all of their possessions just so their families had enough to eat. As the winter months passed, the crime, the profiteering, and the hardship of trying to survive began to turn the people of Philadelphia against the British.

The French Alliance

While the British and American armies stayed in winter quarters, dramatic events took place in Paris. When the American rebellion began, France could not risk joining the rebels until it was clear what was going on in

While the British lived well in Philadelphia, the patriots at Valley Forge suffered from scarcity. A soldier's simple possessions; pewter spoon, cup, and knife.

Benjamin Franklin

Benjamin Franklin was born in Boston in 1706. He went to school for a short time before going to work. In 1723 he went to Philadelphia. He had only one Dutch dollar and one copper shilling in his pocket. Yet he had so much talent and energy that seven years later, at the age of 24, he owned and published a large newspaper, the *Pennsylvania Gazette*.

Franklin had great curiosity. Before the Revolutionary War he founded a debating club, a library, Philadelphia's first fire company, and a school academy. He also became interested in science and inventions. His experiments with electricity made him famous in America and Europe.

He entered politics as a clerk to the Pennsylvania Assembly in 1736. From that time until the beginning of the Revolutionary War Franklin worked to make the American colonies stronger. Among many accomplishments his efforts led to the repeal of the Stamp Act. He was a member of the Second Continental Congress and helped write the Declaration of Independence.

When Congress appointed men to travel to France to negotiate a treaty, Franklin was one of three men chosen. He boarded a small American warship on October 27, 1776, and set sail for France. He knew that if British warships captured his ship, he would probably be taken to London, tried for treason, and hanged. The 70-year-old man acted as if that possibility did not worry him. During the voyage he spent his time happily studying the ocean.

America. French leaders were not certain that the rebels seriously wanted independence from Great Britain. They also worried that the rebel cause might collapse in the face of British fighting strength. So, France decided to help the rebels in secret but not to join with the Americans in public.

Benjamin Franklin arrived in France in December 1776. Congress had given Franklin and two other Americans, Arthur Lee and Silas Deane, the job of negotiating an alliance with France. Franklin was very popular in France. French society appreciated Franklin's

In the fall of 1776 Benjamin Franklin sailed to France aboard the USS *Reprisal*.

scientific discoveries, his intelligence, and his wit. French Foreign Minister Charles Vergennes quickly decided that among the three Americans, Franklin was the one to work with.

For almost a year Vergennes and Franklin worked secretly to help the rebel cause. Because of their efforts American warships visited French ports for weapons and supplies. They departed the ports to attack British ships in nearby waters. The Hortalez & Cie company ran a booming business that sent supplies to the rebels. French warships escorted merchant ships that carried Hortalez & Cie supplies to the rebel armies. As a result, many of the vital supplies used by the American soldiers in 1777 came from France.

British leaders knew that the French were helping the rebels. A British diplomat complained to Vergennes, "It is a fact, sir, a part of the force of this country is directed against us." But there was little the British could do to prevent the French from helping the Americans because France was officially at peace with England.

Franklin got along very well with French society leaders.

Franklin knew that if he showed the French how much the rebels needed French help, he would not be able to negotiate a good deal. He also knew that the French feared that America and Great Britain might make a peace. So, Franklin acted as if an alliance with France was not really important. He also pretended that the rebels were interested in working out a peaceful end to the war with Great Britain.

News that Burgoyne had surrendered at Saratoga and that Washington had attacked the British at Germantown persuaded French leaders to think about joining the rebels openly. Vergennes thought that Burgoyne's defeat might cause the British to offer peace to the rebels. Because of the way Franklin acted, Vergennes thought that Franklin would accept. In a secret French meeting Vergennes said, "Events have surprised us, they have marched more rapidly than we could have expected."

The French king, Louis XVI, wanted to hurry to make an alliance with the Americans. On December 17, 1777,

French authorities told Franklin that France had decided to recognize American independence. On January 8, 1778, Vergennes told Franklin that France was ready to make a formal, open alliance. It was a tremendous offer. Franklin had played his role brilliantly to get the French to make the offer.

France offered America a military alliance that would begin as soon as war broke out between France and England. Everyone knew that such a war would happen soon. When it did begin, the rebels had to pledge themselves to help France defend its colonies in the West Indies. Also, the rebels had to promise not to make a peace with the British unless the French agreed. In

The king of France, Louis XVI, formally meets the American diplomat, Benjamin Franklin.

return, France guaranteed American independence and promised to keep fighting until America won its independence. France also kept open the likelihood that Spain would someday enter the war on the side of the French and Americans.

At first, the Americans and the French tried to keep the alliance secret. Then on March 20, 1778, King Louis XVI called Franklin and the other American diplomats to his court. By his act the king was formally recognizing the rebels. He was sending a message to everyone that France supported the rebel cause. The king told Franklin, "Firmly assure Congress of my friendship; I hope that this will be for the good of both nations."

Franklin replied, "Your Majesty may count on the gratitude of Congress and its faithful observance of the pledges it now takes."

Before news of the French offer of an alliance reached Congress, a British offer arrived. Burgoyne's defeat had caused Lord North to change his policy. Early in 1778 North presented Parliament with a plan to end the war. The plan became know as the "Conciliatory Propositions" (conciliatory means to make peace between warring groups). The Conciliatory Propositions smoothed over almost all of the problems between the rebels and Great Britain. It even agreed that Parliament did not have the right to tax the American colonies. North proposed that there should be an immediate meeting between diplomats on both sides. North added that there was "so much affection left in [America] toward [Great Britain] that barely to enter on a discussion is half the business."

At the time Congress received the Conciliatory Propositions, the war was not going well. Congress had divided into factions that argued with one another. Washington's army was suffering at Valley Forge. The British held the two biggest American cities, New York and Philadelphia. The Royal Navy blockaded the coast. There had been no news from Franklin for almost a year.

The leadership of George Washington and the determination of his army were key to the survival of the rebel cause until France became an American ally.

Yet every congressman was against North's proposal. Congress did not trust the British. Congressmen believed that even if it agreed to a peace, soon the British "lust of domination" would cause Great Britain to attack America again. Congress rejected the Conciliatory Propositions. Then, on May 2, 1778, Congress received the French offer of alliance. Congress ratified (approved) the French Alliance two days later.

The French alliance was the decisive turning point in the war. France was the greatest nation in Europe. Its population of 25 million people was three times larger than the population of Great Britain and ten times larger that the population of the United States. The French army was much bigger than the British army. The French navy was about equal to the British navy. All that strength joined the rebel side. Without the French alliance the Americans could not have won the war.

But France did not actually enter the fighting until June 1778. It would take even longer for French ships and soldiers to arrive off the American coast and lend help to the rebels. Until the French came, the rebels had to continue the war alone.

Chronology

December 12, 1776: As the British occupy nearby New Jersey, the Continental Congress flees Philadelphia for Baltimore. After George Washington wins victories at Trenton and Princeton, Congress returns to Philadelphia early in 1777.

December 27, 1776: Congress grants George Washington important additional powers.

June 1777: British General Howe tries to force George Washington and his Continental Army into battle in New Jersey, but Washington avoids him.

July 1777: Learning that Burgoyne's army is winning victories to the north, General Howe decides to move his army in the opposite direction to capture Philadelphia. This decision shows that Howe and Burgoyne will not cooperate during the 1777 campaign.

July 11, 1777: General Howe's army boards ships in New York to go by sea and launch an invasion of Philadelphia. Unfavorable winds and a roundabout route force the soldiers and their horses to spend 47 days on board ship. They finally land in Maryland on August 25.

September 11, 1777: The British attack the Continentals at Brandywine Creek, near Philadelphia. The more experienced British defeat the Americans but do not destroy the rebel army.

September 21, 1777: The British sneak up on sleeping American soldiers camped at Paoli, near Philadelphia, and kill, capture, and drive off the surprised rebels.

September 26, 1777: The British march into Philadelphia without a fight.

October 4, 1777: Washington's army surprises the British before sunrise at Germantown and almost defeats them. But when American troops fire at their own side by accident, it causes a panic, and the Americans retreat from the field.

November 1777: The British force the Americans to abandon two forts on the Delaware River, opening Philadelphia to British ships.

December 17, 1777: Learning of the American victory at Saratoga, France recognizes American independence.

December 1777: George Washington's army goes into winter quarters at Valley Forge, Pennsylvania.

May 1778: The Continental Congress receives and ratifies France's offer to form an alliance.

Glossary

The word "cabal" has an interesting history. By the time of the Revolutionary War it was known to mean a group plotting secretly. But in 1667 England's King Charles II chose five men to conduct foreign policy in secret: Clifford, Ashley, Buckingham, Arlington, and Lauderdale. When the names of the five officials became known to the public, people thought it was sinister that their initials spelled CABAL.

ALLIANCE: agreement between two nations to fight on the same side in a war

BLOCKADE: an effort to patrol the ocean to keep trading ships from entering or leaving a port

CABAL: a small group who plot together for a secret purpose, usually to get more power in a government

CONTINENTAL: referring to troops in the American army

COURT MARTIAL: trial by a military, or martial, court

DESERTION: leaving the army or navy without permission

FLANK: one side of an army

HESSIANS: hired German soldiers who fought for the British in the Revolutionary War. The Americans called all German mercenaries "Hessians."

LOYALIST: an American who wanted America to remain under British rule; also called a Tory

MANEUVER: a planned movement of troops and equipment to accomplish a military goal

MERCENARIES: soldiers who get paid to fight for a foreign country

MUTINY: an attempt by soldiers or sailors to overthrow their officers

QUARTERMASTER: officer responsible for supplying an army with quarters (living space), clothing, and equipment. The Continental Army had a separate department for supplying food.

RALLY: to encourage and reorganize soldiers who are about to lose their nerve and rout (run away) from a battlefield

TERM OF ENLISTMENT: the agreed amount of time a soldier or sailor will stay in the army or navy

WINTER QUARTERS: where armies stayed during the winter

Further Resources

Books:

Boatner, Mark M., III. *Encyclopedia of the American Revolution*. Mechanicsburg, PA: Stackpole Books, 1994.

Daugherty, James. *Poor Richard*. Lakeville, CT: Grey Castle Press, 1991. A biography of Benjamin Franklin

Franklin, Benjamin. *Autobiography & Other Writings*. New York: Oxford University Press, 1999.

Fritz, Jean. *Why Not, Lafayette?* New York: G.P. Putnam's Sons, 1999.

Hughes, Libby. *Valley Forge*. Parsippany, NJ: Silver Burdett, 1993.

Meltzer, Milton. *Benjamin Franklin: The New American*. New York: Franklin Watts, 1988.

Rankin, Hugh F., ed. *Narratives of the American Revolution as told by a young sailor, a home-sick surgeon, a French volunteer, and a German general's wife.* Chicago: Lakeside Press, 1976. The homesick surgeon describes the winter at Valley Forge.

Scheer, George F. and Hugh F. Rankin. *Rebels & Redcoats: The American Revolution through the Eyes of Those Who Fought & Lived It.* New York: Da Capo Press, 1987.

Young, Robert. *The Real Patriots of the American Revolution*. Parsippany, NJ: Silver Burdett, 1996.

Websites:

http://library.thinkquest.org/10966/
The Revolutionary War—A Journey Towards Freedom

ushistory.org/march/index.html
Virtual Marching Tour of the American

Revolutionhttp://www.pbs.org/ktca/liberty/game/index.html
The Road to Revolution—A Revolutionary Game

http://www.pbs.org/ktca/liberty/chronicle/index.html
Chronicle of the Revolution
Read virtual newspapers of the Revolutionary era

http://www.nps.gov/vafo
Official website of Valley Forge National Historical Park

A Place to Visit:

Valley Forge National Historical Park, Valley Forge, Pennsylvania

About the Authors

James R. Arnold has written more than 20 books on military history topics and contributed to many others. Roberta Wiener has coauthored several books with Mr. Arnold and edited numerous educational books, including a children's encyclopedia. They live and farm in Virginia.

Set Index

Bold numbers refer to volumes; *italics* refer to illustrations

Acknowledgments

Architect of the Capitol: 12–13, 50–51,

Author's collection: 30, 45, 48T

Ballou's Pictorial: 64–65

Anne S. K. Brown Military Collection, John Hay Library, Brown University, Providence, Rhode Island: Front cover, 54, 56–57, 66–67

Independence National Historical Park: 17T, 21B, 24T, 24B, 29, 31, 34, 44

Library of Congress: 8, 20, 22–23, 25T, 25B, 26B, 27, 28B, 38–39, 40, 48–49, 52–53, 55, 58

National Archives: 6–7, 10, 11, 16, 19, 21T, 59, 63

The George C. Neumann Collection, a gift of the Sun Company to Valley Forge National Historical Park, 1978, 60

U.S. Government Printing Office: 9 by Don Troiani, 26T, 28T

U.S. Marine Corps, Washington D.C.: 36 *The Evacuation of Billingsport 2 October 1777,* by Charles Waterhouse

U.S. Naval Historical Center, Washington, D.C.: 14–15, 17B, 37, 41, 42–43, 62

Valley Forge Historical Society: Title page and 46–47, *The March to Valley Forge,* by W. B. T. Trego, 32–33 *The Battle of Paoli,* by Xavier della Gatta

Maps by Jerry Malone